The Right Frame

a consideration of the
right and wrong methods of framing pictures

by Henry Heydenryk

LYONS & BURFORD, PUBLISHERS

By the same author:

THE ART AND HISTORY OF FRAMES

James H. Heineman, Inc., 1963

Copyright © 1964 by James H. Heineman

ALL RIGHTS RESERVED. No part of this book may be reproduced
in any manner without the express written consent of the
publisher, except in the case of brief excerpts in critical
reviews and articles. All inquiries should be addressed
to: Lyons & Burford, 31 West 21 Street, New York, NY 10010.

Printed in the United States of America

10 9 8 7 6 5 4 3 2 1

Design by Norma Levarie

Library of Congress Cataloging-in-Publication Data

Heydenryk, Henry.
    The right frame : a consideration of the right and wrong methods
  of framing pictures / by Henry Heydenryk.
        p.   cm.
      Originally published: New York : Heineman, 1963.
      Includes bibliographical references.
      ISBN 1-55821-266-3
      1. Picture frames and framing.   I. Title.
  N8550.H43   1993
  749'.7—dc20
                                               93-1619
                                                 CIP

We are pleased to thank W. & J. Sloane and Company, N.Y.C., for the pictures appearing on pages 63 and 65 which were taken in their showrooms; Miss Gloria Vanderbilt for the pictures appearing on pages 53 and 87 which were taken in her home; Dr. Bob Jones for the picture appearing on page 14; Dr. G. Wagner for permission to reproduce his painting by George Bullman appearing on pages 72 and 73; Mr. Alfredo Valente for the picture appearing on page 54; The Cheatham Foundation for permission to show *The Pomegranate Heart* appearing on page 86; The Rijksmuseum, Amsterdam, for the reproductions of Johan Vermeer's *De Brief* appearing on page 16, and Giovanni Bellini's *Madonna and Child* appearing on page 15; Miss Patricia Harvey of the J. Walter Thompson Company, N.Y.C., for the interior appearing on page 84; The Boston Museum of Fine Arts for permission to reproduce Copley's painting of Mrs. Ezekiel Goldthwait; and Mr. John Davis, Sausaulito, California, for the pictures appearing on pages 60 and 62 which were taken in his home.

Contents

This book is generously supplied
with irreverent scribbles
by FREDERICK FRANCK

The Right Frame

Foreword

There are few aspects of interior design where there is a greater need for sound information and expert advice than in the presentation of art works. The framing, hanging and lighting of paintings, drawings and wall decorations of all kinds may establish the atmosphere of a room or a house, enhance or depreciate the quality of the pictures and signify the owner's taste. It has been my experience that many people are casual, careless or uninformed about picture framing. I feel that this book by Henry Heydenryk, a professional of experience and judgment, makes a contribution in an area where reference works are limited.

Whether or not you agree with G. K. Chesterton who said: "Art is limitation; the essence of every picture is the frame," there is no gainsaying the importance of this corollary to art. The picture framer's skill is a precise one, as invaluable as it is usually anonymous and unappreciated. The perfect frame is so suitable that it attracts no attention to itself.

The function of the frame is to protect the picture, to enhance it without entering into competition and to make a transition between the limits of the picture and the wall it occupies or the composition with which it is involved. Aesthetically the frame should complement the subject matter it surrounds. Picture frames should be chosen with all these elements in mind, and they are ably discussed by Mr. Heydenryk in this monograph which is dedicated to the whole concept of framing.

Fine picture frames are as well-designed and as durable as fine furniture. Quality or the lack of it is readily obvious in a picture frame, and to compromise is to defeat the purpose of art. It is wisdom to go to a specialist for the framing of good pictures and to take with you some understanding of the nature and scope of framing, as well as definitive knowledge of the wall and the room where your picture will hang. As well as complementing the subject matter of the painting, the frame should bear some relationship to other elements in the room, especially when it comes to scale, color and style.

Picture frames are affected by changing fashions in interior architecture and home furnishings as well as by new styles, techniques and approaches in painting. Modern painting has accounted for many changes in framemaking—the use of new materials, new textures and a simplification of moldings. Many modern artists have exhibited interest in the framing of their works to the degree of designing their own frames.

While a frame contemporary with the period of a painting is a safe assumption, the frame must be appropriate to the picture as well as historically correct. It is also possible to frame pictures satisfactorily in frames which derive from differing periods, if the effect is pleasing and other requirements of framing are fulfilled. In the popular "picture walls," instituted by interior designers to remedy the architectural monotony of long rectangular-shaped rooms in many modern apartment buildings, frames of various periods and styles can be juxtaposed effectively.

New framing of old pictures can give a new quality to interiors. Frames can become as dated as antimacassars, and Victorian hangovers in contemporary interiors are out of place. The quality of a room can be changed by updating the picture frames. Good pictures deserve the proper mounting, and a fine painting can be obliterated by an improper frame.

Interior designers will find Mr. Heydenryk's treatise especially useful, for the picture frame is an important adjunct in the creation of an effect often overlooked. One also hopes that professional framers will be spurred to new originality in their offerings by this volume, for we are often limited by what is available. The field offers unexplored possibilities for the designer.

For the collector or the owner of paintings, the study of this manual will give a new appreciation of his possessions. When choosing a frame, a primary goal should be the furthering of the artist's intention. If you accomplish this subjectively, the experience will give your picture new meaning for you.

William Pahlmann, F.A.I.D.

Introduction

A strange paradox exists today in the world of art.

On the one hand, it is evident that there has been a remarkable increase in the number of people interested in oil paintings, watercolors, fine photographs and other types of pictures. On the other hand, it is astonishing that only a small proportion of these growing art lovers has any real concept of how to frame and hang pictures to achieve the best possible effect from what the artist has created.

A recent profile about me in *The New Yorker* magazine opened with these words: "Of all the long-suffering and self-effacing vice-regents of the arts whose primary function is to add lustre to somebody or something else—the accompanist to the soloist, the stage designer to the play, the second fiddle to the first fiddle—hardly any are less often honored by even incidental notice than the picture framer."

My colleagues and I are naturally concerned over this lack of understanding, but we take for granted that we have to undertake a certain amount of education to make the importance of proper framing better understood. We are concerned also with another aspect of the situation, mentioned or implied in several places in the article, that the selection of appropriate picture frames is either overlooked entirely, left to chance or else so imbued with fetishism that the pictures themselves become secondary to the frames.

It would be unfair to ascribe the situation to the rapidly growing body of amateur painters and collectors, who could be excused for never having been informed about the role frames should play in art. In fact, the very need for this book arose from a minor crisis in the art world itself. A number of years ago, I was called upon by the Virginia Museum of Fine Art, in Richmond, to help solve a problem. The curators were so discouraged by the poorly framed entries of participants in the competitions for the Virginia Biennials that they asked me to prepare an exhibit. Their objective was to demonstrate the need for proper framing to prevent artists from partially destroying the very canvases they had created by using poor judgment and taste in framing.

Out of this situation grew an exhibit entitled, "Framing, Right and Wrong."

Since that time, the exhibit has traveled to hundreds of museums in almost every state in the Union. Its popularity is attested to by the fact that it is regularly booked ahead for a period of two years. It has been well covered by the press; examples have been displayed in magazines; and it has appeared several times on television.

The purpose of this book is to explore, for beginners and established professionals alike, the "rights" and "wrongs" of picture framing, both in detail and in the broadest aspects of the subject. Since such intangibles as *taste, preference* and *tradition* enter into the matter of framing—as in the case of any other area of the arts—there can be no absolute rights and wrongs. Some will question my selection of examples reproduced on the following pages. Others will perhaps take issue with my reasons for recommending certain types of frames for specific pictures and rejecting others. But I am firmly convinced that the contents of this book, the consideration of the many aspects of selecting appropriate frames, will go a long way toward providing fine art with one important element of support that has been seriously lacking.

This is *not* a "How to" book. It will not show you how to make new picture frames, or even how to restore or decorate old ones. There are already several thoroughly detailed books in print on that subject. The objective of this book is, rather, to establish the concept of the picture frame in its rightful place, to stimulate interest in, and thoughtful consideration of, the selection of frames, and to serve as an aesthetic guide to better framing.

What is a frame?

The original "picture frame" was simply an opening in the forest foliage through which some caveman looked forth on a scene appealing enough to capture and hold his attention for perhaps several minutes before he was disconcerted by something else. It is not uncommon today to find such lookout points revered by primitive tribesmen, leaf-framed bowers where traditionally only the chiefs or witch doctors were permitted to sit or crouch in isolated contemplation of the scene at hand.

At some unknown date in ancient history, it became the practice to frame a special setting by constructing a crude doorway of timbers, and later rocks, so that those entering would first have the impression of some natural entity contained within limitations set by man. The natural evolution was from rough slabs of stone, to the carved and massive doorways of the Egyptians, and ultimately to the arch, first perfected by the Assyrians around the seventh century B.C.

The important point here is that the picture frame, as a distinct element, originated with this whole concept of directing a viewer's eyes through an attractively designed opening toward a scene entirely contained within the focal point of that opening.

It can be said, in effect, that the entrance to your home, an attractive doorway into a dining room, or a rose-clustered trellis at the near end of a garden are all frames. The same is true of a decorative fireplace, the proscenium of a theater or the archway separating the nave from the rest of a church.

This concept of viewing a scene through some kind of portal was actually carried over into artists' interpretations of early picture frames. As Edward Landon says in the introduction to his book on methods of making and finishing picture frames, "The earliest examples of frame-like decorations or borders bear a great resemblance to door frames. They were composed of two columns surmounted by a connecting entablature and this form persisted into the 15th century. Even the decorations painted by the artists around the edges of pictures before the introduction of movable frames were similar in form."*

Going back to the earliest sculptured reliefs from Egypt, Persia, Phoenicia and other ancient lands, we see examples of this kind of an attempt by artists to contain their work within a border. Many of these reliefs were framed by carved representations of temple doors or other formal openings actually in use at the time. Movable picture frames, as we know them today, date from the Italian Renaissance.

What is a frame? In *Webster's New International Dictionary*, it is described generally as "A kind of open case or structure made for admitting, enclosing, or supporting things, as that which encloses or contains a window, door, picture, etc.; that on which anything is held or stretched. . . . An enclosing border, esp. an ornamental one. . . ."

Frames can be as small as a coin, to encase a miniature portrait, or as large as the longest room, to set off a huge, extravagant mural. They can

---

*Edward Landon, *Picture Framing* (Tudor Publishing Company, New York, 1962).

be as flat as a sheet of paper, as deep as an office desk. There is no limitation as to shape—oblong, square, round, oval, triangular, pentagonal, hexagonal, octagonal or even so misshapen as to defy geometric classification.

For practical purposes, the components and elements of a standard picture frame can be broken down as follows:

1 MOLDING. This is the basic element. Moldings can be classified broadly into four categories: flat or angular, single-curved, multicurved and compound. The latter may be a combination of curves and angles, or sometimes may be a combination of moldings within moldings.

2 DECORATION. This may or may not be present on a molding, in the form of carving, scratching, combing, metal or stone ornaments, or other artistic work that makes the overall design more complex. Many frames have plaster or composition ornaments or are decorated with veneer.

3 FINISH. There are two basic types of finishes: ones that are almost invisible, such as varnish, shellac or wax, that are applied for purposes of *protecting* the frame; ones that are meant to be seen, such as white or colored casein paste paint, bronze powders, gold, silver or bronze metal leaf, or other coloring matter for *decorative* purposes.

4 MATS. These are flat pieces of cardboard, pressed wood or other material, used within the outer molding or frame to set off the picture and somewhat isolate it. Mats may be plain or decorated, colored or natural,

uncovered or covered with some attractive material such as rough cloth or fine paper. Not all frames have mats, but when this element is used it may be pencil-thin or extremely wide, depending upon the nature of the picture and the purpose of the mat.

5   BACKING. Frequently confused with "mounting," the backing is that part of the frame used, when necessary, as a support for the picture itself. Oil paintings seldom require backing, but delicate woodcuts or old engravings will need them for support. The usual cardboard or mat board will deteriorate and discolor with age, which then may also stain the paper of lithographs, drawings and other graphic material. A backing, therefore, should be 100 per cent rag content. Pictures should be attached to this board with inert paper "hinges," similar to those used in stamp albums. (*Note:* Many valuable pictures have been permanently stained by the improper use of various gummed tapes.)

6   GLASS. This element is seen most often with watercolors, pastels, engravings and other art work that does not have any natural protection on the surface against dust and grime. Oil paintings seldom require glass, except when in such ancient or poor condition that they could be ruined by the smallest accumulations of dust or dirt. Whenever and wherever used with pictures, glass should be all but invisible, and so lighted that reflections do not spoil the effect of the picture itself. New types of glare-proof glass, though somewhat more expensive than the ordinary kind, offer one method for solving the problem. However, nonreflecting glass has the disadvantage of having a slight opacity. This quality makes little difference on a black-and-white print or a strong watercolor, but it can slightly blur a picture whose definition is not sharp to begin with, and to some degree it flattens out delicate colorings.

7   INSERTS. Often called "liners," these elements are the ones beneath and within the outer moldings. They are used for a number of purposes: to give depth and dimension to the molding; to form an extra, decorative border next to the picture; to serve as the separation between color and

pattern of the painting and the frame; to reduce the size of a frame that is slightly too large for the picture itself.

8 BACKING PAPER. Many pictures, particularly those that require glass on the front, are sealed in the back with a sheet of strong paper, tightly glued to the frame and cut so that the edges are not visible. Backing paper simply protects the picture from dust and to a limited degree from changes in humidity. It is also sometimes useful for recording the date of the picture, place of purchase, cost, etc.

9 HANGERS. The hanging unit on the back of a picture frame should be properly placed and adjusted, so that not only will the picture retain an even position on the wall, but there will be no lopsided stress on the frame itself. Unusually large, or heavy, frames should be wired so that the wire is attached to two separate screw eyes, positioned about one-third of the way down from the top edge of the frame. (*Note:* Some thin frames can be given extra strength by stringing an additional wire tautly between two screw eyes on the vertical sides of the frame—or, if necessary, running from top to bottom.) So-called mirror hangers that are attached by one or more screws and that lie flat against the back of a frame, are preferable for heavy pictures.

10 FITTING STRIPS. Wooden or metal strips may be attached to the outer edge of a canvas or panel for protection. They should project approximately ⅛″ above the painted surface so that the frame will rest on these strips and not press on the painting. This prevents damage to the surface due to pressure or friction and preserves the canvas from unnecessary wear.

Caroline Keck's book, *How to Take Care of Your Pictures,* is probably the best work written on the subject. The American Federation of Arts also discusses this subject in the Winter, 1963 issue of its quarterly.

A brief historical sketch

In ancient times, the only real frames that existed were those used for hand mirrors, or for setting off certain pieces of jewelry. One German authority stated that paintings were sometimes "framed" by being placed, free-standing, on decorated stands in wealthy homes long before the time of Christ. His findings, however, are based on illustrations within some surviving Pompeiian wall paintings; and there are no existing relics of such stands as evidence.

We must therefore begin any realistic appraisal of the history of frames with the Middle Ages. Up until that time, oil painting had been considered not an independent art, but basically an *architectural* element. Then, in the thirteenth century, with the beginning of the Italian Renaissance. panel paintings began to be in evidence—not only in Italy, but throughout Europe. The earliest panel paintings had frames only in that the pictures were executed on the flat, slightly hollowed, surfaces of wooden sheets.

The raised rim, often painted or decorated as a separate element, then served as the frame.

The next natural step in the development was for artists to paint a picture on a panel and then affix to it a surrounding rim of heavier wood. At first, the real purpose was to reinforce the picture and to prevent the thin panel from warping, with a consequent cracking of the painted surface.

In the late fifteenth century, Italian painters began to look upon their work as an independent art, no longer wedded to architecture, and significant enough for development in its own right. Many of the Italian master painters of the day became accomplished frame-makers. It was only logical that framing itself should then develop as a serious art in itself.

With the sixteenth century came an important milestone in framing. Patrons of the arts, who formerly had sponsored artists only for creating "great" works in cathedrals, churches and occasionally public buildings, now began to hunger for art in their own homes. They began to commission portraits and allegorical representations, or look for other subjects of personal interest, which could then be framed and hung in their own halls. In Italy the rich merchants and nobles, like the Medici in Florence or the Gonzaga in Mantua, poured such fortunes into the purchase of this kind of art that the demand for fine frames launched a thriving new business. Many painters, pressed with work, could do little more than sketch out the desired designs and pass along the frame-making assignments to their apprentices or to outside artisans.

It has been generally accepted that the sixteenth century in Italy inspired some of the finest frames ever designed and made.

It is rather remarkable that the frames of this period exhibited such great taste and restraint, for the whole concept of framing at the beginning of the Italian Renaissance had stemmed from the way painting had been incorporated into architecture. The resulting frames, therefore, were almost literal reproductions of the niches into which the art had been placed. When removed from an ecclesiastical setting, frames that tried to reproduce architectural elements were so heavy and so elaborate against, say, an ordinary wall, that the paintings within were completely overpowered.

The great masters of the sixteenth century somehow managed to avoid this exaggeration, designing frames that were completely harmonious with the paintings contained within them. But it was too good to last. In the late sixteenth century, frame-makers seemed determined to push their art for all it was worth. Moldings not only became elaborately carved, but often were cluttered with "foreign objects," such as jewels, carved chunks of semiprecious stone and bits of mirrored glass. All over Europe, fads began to spring up, as frame-makers tried to outdo each other by adding tortoise-shell, ivory, mother-of-pearl and many another attention-getting substance.

It is interesting to note that the best of these elaborate frames—though too busy and restless for pictures—are not at all unappropriate for *mirrors*, where there is no constant image to cause interference. Venice, an important center for producing mirrors, was also the origin of many of the frames that we now classify as too overpowering and ornate for even the strongest oil paintings.

The moral here is that the frame's *purpose* is all-important to its design.

In the seventeenth century, Italian frames became somewhat more subdued, but leadership in the decorative arts passed over into France, where it was solidly entrenched until the time of the French Revolution. French frames of the period were imitated all over Europe, starting with the reign of Louis XIII (1610–1643) and to a tremendous degree during the Golden Age of France in the reign of Louis XIV (1643–1715). Now, too, picture framing became firmly established as a separate craft. The noted Paris guilds were developed; standards were set and steadfastly controlled; and artisans concentrated on specialization. The frame-maker was a specialist within the already accepted profession of the cabinetmaker. Because of standardization, there is a certain sameness, however, in Louis XIV frames.

In the meantime, the Dutch were also perfecting the art of picture framing. While many of their designs were variations on the French, they did

*Suiting a frame to the period can be accomplished with
either an original or a reproduction. The altar-like Gothic frame is a
recently made reproduction of one made in the fifteenth century.*

Frame is a sixteenth-century original from the Italian Renaissance.

Frames of the period. Above, Dutch seventeenth-century frame for Vermeer's The Letter. *Right, a Chippendale-inspired original for Copley's* Mrs. Ezekiel Goldthwait.

contribute some unique features. One was the use of exotic woods, such as ebony or mahogany, imported through the globe-encircling network of Dutch trade. Another was the development of a type known as the "border" frame perfected in the sixteenth century as the Lowlands interpretation of the Italian molding.

Often, throughout history, the very technique of making a molding has developed such artistry, or perhaps artisanship, that the frame has ended up half swallowing the painting. A talented Amsterdam goldsmith, Johan Lutma, for example, perfected a type of carved frame that in itself was a beauty to behold, with intricate little impressions of sea animals, birds, flowers and other wildlife—all in high relief on a fairly flat molding. The problem that resulted with the popularization of this type of frame—and more markedly with frames carved by less skillful artists than Lutma—was that many a fine painting found its strength weakened by an encircling array of trivia that distracted the eye.

The splendor and elegance of decoration reached a new height in France during the reign of Louis XV (1723–1774) as the decorative arts dominated the fine arts and frames became used everywhere. They appeared not only around pictures, but on fire screens, in fabric designs, as elements of huge tapestries, for title pages of books and even around commercial announcements. Swirls and undulations and leafy designs were found wherever a decoration was called for, and in many places where it was not.

Shortly after the middle of the eighteenth century, this kind of exuberant design gave way to the austere simplicity of neoclassicism, which spread quickly from its beginnings in Rome after the discovery of the buried cities of Herculaneum and Pompeii. In France, the new style was generally referred to as Louis XVI, continuing until the beginning of the French Revolution in 1789, after which France's influence over the arts went into a severe and prolonged decline.

Under Napoleon, at the beginning of the nineteenth century, frame-making went into another stage of development during the Empire period.

Much of the earlier classicism was retained, but there was a decided uniformity of design in most areas of art. The result was the precise, severe "scoop molding" with plaster-cast ornamentation. The Empire frame is marked by perfect symmetry and precise, harsh detail. While this kind of frame certainly has its place with many realistic paintings, Napoleon's overzealous championship of it even now is being felt in Paris. The curators of the Louvre are still trying to replace most of the Empire frames in which Napoleon insisted the exhibits there should be hung.

This classic example of misframing was so great that Gertrude Stein was once moved to write about it:

"The Louvre at first was only gold frames to me gold frames which were rather glorious, and looking out of the window of the Louvre with the gold frames being all gold behind within was very glorious. I always like, as well as liked looking out of windows in museums. It is more complete, looking out of windows in museums than looking out of windows any-where else...."

Many another visitor to the Louvre has found it more pleasant to look out of the window than at all those gold frames!

Napoleon was not alone in this predisposition for uniformity. Many a more knowledgeable art authority than the Emperor fell into the pitfall of disregarding each painting as an individual work. Louis XIII and Louis XIV frames were copied and turned out in assembly-line fashion as the nineteenth century progressed. Imitations of the carvings of the seven-teenth century were so mechanically cast in plaster that they resembled iron. Bright gilding continued to be in vogue, so brash that it completely drew the eye away from the picture within.

Worst of all, it became the accepted practice among patrons of the arts to house large collections of paintings in *identical* frames, regardless of the subject matter, composition or other elements concerned.

It was inevitable that eventually there should be a rebellion.

In the latter part of the nineteenth century, a group of artists began to defy the framing regimentation of the public and private galleries. They reexamined the function of the picture frame and found that the entire concept had long since become hideously deformed. Up until the 1870's, changes in taste and outlook had undergone a gradual metamorphosis, from good to bad to worse. Now the situation had become so intolerable that the artists concerned simply rejected everything that had gone before and started from the beginning. It was like a return to the Middle Ages, when framing was an architectural element and a small group of artists realized that there was something wrong with the concept.

The result was the development of the Impressionist frame, often a simple molding in white or white softened by small amounts of coloring. A few artists, notably Seurat and Degas, viewed the frame with such nat-ural suspicion that they took to using simple, flat moldings, on which they

painted and speckled colors similar to the ones used on the canvases themselves, in effect, extending the painting outward a few inches.

America was spared a good many of the atrocities of overframing found
in Europe for a good many years, mainly because there were few artisans
and little machinery or tools for executing the elaborate frames in France
and Italy. Many Early American frames were effective because of their
stark simplicity, bordering pictures which in themselves bore the primitive
stamp. But the floodgates were opened in America, as elsewhere, during the
Victorian period.

"The frame-makers who constructed the monstrosities of the Victorian
era," wrote artist Edward Landon, "were not content to put one heavily
embellished gold frame around a picture of 'The Stag at Bay' or something
similar, but three or four. This birthday cake was then enclosed in a glass-

covered, plush-lined, mahogany shadow-box. This was presumably for protection, but its need is a mystery since the interiors of that time were heavily shaded and hermetically sealed anyway."

After 1900, partly as a reaction against the extremes of Victorianism, picture frames tended to become less cluttered. As concerns geometrical paintings in particular, the frames became reduced to little more than narrow bands. This trend might have continued almost until the present day had not the Paris Exposition of 1925 sparked a renewed interest in "Modern Art." After that date, the narrow moldings gave way to frames that had more substance, and that began to bear some relationship to the pictures for which they were intended. In the 1930's, France, Belgium and Holland produced not a few talented frame-makers who began to create designs for the exciting new schools of painting that were blooming on all sides.

After the tragic interruption caused by World War II, frame-making blossomed once again as many old art treasures were removed from their hiding places in war-ravaged lands, and as there sprang up—particularly in the United States—a remarkably strong interest in the arts. Although there are plenty of examples of bad, and tasteless, framing, it is encouraging to note the increase in good framing to be found in many homes and galleries. There is, too, tremendous excitement in current experimentation, in trying out new materials and textures and methods—not just for the sake of innovation, but to provide new art styles with frames that enhance their values.

It is refreshing to feel, and to be convinced, that the art of framing is on the ascendancy.

A considered approach

to the

nature of the frame

"The framing of a painting or drawing is a *presentation* of that painting or drawing to the best advantage. It is a means of defining and emphasizing the picture's area in relation to the larger area of the room. It should enhance, embellish, complement and emphasize the picture. It should never overpower the subject. The frame acts as a sort of impresario, the picture remains the star performer, whether it's an original Botticelli or a Gauguin reprint."

This statement was made some years ago by Van Day Truex, a painter in his own right and former president of the Parsons School of Design, in an article on how to frame and hang pictures. What Mr. Truex was concerned with in part—and what this chapter is devoted to—focuses on the *nature* of the frame. It is easy enough to define the physical makeup of a frame, and to isolate the various elements that go into it, but the interpretation is another matter entirely. Your overall impression of any specific frame will probably fit into one of the following three classifications:

1 The frame will be sharp and distinct, setting off the picture with clearly defined lines.

2 The frame will blend with the picture or the design, its definition slightly out of focus or soft, its style and design almost unnoticed. ·

3 The frame will generally fit into the second category, but there will be certain sharply defined features—perhaps in the mat or the insert.

Selecting the proper frame for a picture, while it is guided by certain factors of taste and style that will be discussed later, must be considered just as personal as choosing furniture for your living room or a major item of clothing. Too many people just "go out and buy a frame" whose inner dimensions are correct for the picture and whose price is within what they feel to be a reasonable budget. Surprisingly few do what any stylish woman does when buying a hat: try six, ten, a dozen different frames *on the picture* before making a decision.

A reliable frame-maker will not simply show you samples of mats and chevrons of molding and expect you to make an on-the-spot choice. He will have on hand a wide selection of *complete* frames, to help you come to a tasteful decision. He will also help you to avoid the old myths that "all oils should be enclosed in gilded frames" or that "watercolors invariably require a wide mat to set them off against the background" or that "graphic prints are not properly framed unless bordered by a black molding and a white mat."

There are, of course, thousands of different types and styles of frames—enough to confuse even an accomplished decorator. However, the confusion is diminished if you bear in mind that there are only six basic categories to select from:

1 Simple, wood frames, whose attractiveness de-

pends mainly on the kind of wood grain, its color, finish and texture.

2 Frames whose moldings are contoured with composition, gesso (plaster, or similar), and whose finish is either plain or patterned.

3 Frames finished with gesso, but with additional carving, gilding or other ornamentation.

4 Hand-carved reproductions of frames from specific periods, such as Italian Renaissance or Louis XIV.

5 Actual antique frames from a major period.

6 Plastic-coated frames, or combinations of plastic, metal and wood.

After selecting a style or period, the next major consideration is one of *proportion*. The width of the frame, on the one hand, has to be substantial enough to suit the size, subject matter and medium of the picture. On the other hand, it must not be so wide as to squash the picture or overpower it. Because of subject matter and palette, many paintings look *larger* or *smaller* than they actually are. They must be framed accordingly.

While it is true that certain periods in the history of art have generated certain types and styles of frames, one popular misconception should be corrected: *the period of the painting or reproduction does not necessarily determine the style of the frame.*

The situation parallels that of the woman going out to buy a new dress (if we may use that old simile again). If she is overweight, she selects colors and styles that minimize the poundage. If she is too thin, she selects a "frame" that will give the reverse effect. Your selection of a frame, and the matting that goes with it, must be influenced by what artists sometimes refer to as the "weight" of the picture itself. This term has nothing to do with the avoirdupois of the picture. Rather, it is concerned with the colors, the strength of the colors and the composition. An oil painting with heavy, dark areas of color would obviously require a different frame from the same subject—even the same square footage of surface—rendered with delicate strokes, or in pastels.

Top, a frame of the Sixties for a recent painting by Frederick Franck,
Shell Patterns. *Right, reproduction of a Spanish Renaissance frame for*
Rouault's Le Chinois *harmonizes with the richness of the subject.*

Braque's Still Life With Grapes *is set off with a wide, flat frame with a carved pattern that echoes the detail in the picture. The plain, narrow insert is appropriate.*

The width of the frame has been mentioned above. Less obvious to the viewer, but of equal importance is the *depth* of the frame, that is, the dimension from the outermost part of the molding to the part that touches the wall.

The nature of the frame is also considerably determined by one fairly down-to-earth factor: the type of material used for the molding. Besides plain or carved wood, the most familiar (though not necessarily the most understood) material is gesso. Gesso, which means "chalk" or "plaster" in Italian, is basically finely ground chalk mixed with a glue solution, that can be readily worked by knowledgeable craftsmen and that dries into a hard, durable finish. Its only real disadvantage is the fact that it tends to be brittle, and hence can be chipped during transportation or storage.

Gesso has been popular down through the centuries in the art world because it is easy to obtain, inexpensive and an extremely flexible medium for artistic creativity. For example, here are a few of the methods of transforming globs of soft gesso into works of art. Gesso can be...

mixed with coloring matter to achieve either a uniform or an uneven stain throughout

surface-colored with gold-leaf gilding or a patina

imprinted with almost any two-dimensional design—from coins to carved symbols to the texture of coarse-grained cloth against the surface

shellacked, glazed and waxed

combed (with an ordinary comb or notched metal) and scratched (with any sharp instrument)

ingrained with foreign objects—metal flakes, glass, sand and so on

carved with an artisan's tools

stippled with a wet brush, branch or other common device

mixed with reinforcing materials (such as asbestos, fiber, rosin) to make a malleable material that can be cast or pressed from molds.

A brief description of the gesso process has been included here, not to try to stimulate do-it-yourself efforts (gesso is highly popular with artists who like to make their own frames, because of its flexibility), but to provide a better understanding of the *nature* of the frame and one of the most familiar materials in its makeup. Understanding the materials helps greatly in determining the best frame for a picture—just as understanding various hardwoods and fabrics does in helping a decorator to select furniture.

One important characteristic of a good picture frame is that it be as durable as fine furniture. It has to be if it is to fulfill its primary practical function: to protect the picture. Despite this durability, there are few old paintings that still retain the original frame. This situation is not so much a result of deterioration or damage as it is a consequence of changing tastes.

Making a frame; applying gesso.

Old Masters were frequently taken out of their original frames and these frames were replaced with some that were more in vogue with a later era. As a result, the artistry of picture framing has been much maligned down through the ages, with fads and crazes taking over the function that should have been exercised by good taste.

More than four decades ago, art critic Peyton Boswell wrote in a magazine article: "Of all the transgressions of good taste and common sense that have been made in the sacred name of art, those connected with the framing of pictures are perhaps the most flagrant. [The United States] especially has been a hard offender. Just as our forbears used to obscure the female form in horrible hoopskirts, so they were wont to ensconce their pictures in heavy, ornate frames and—save the mark!—they even hid away both frame and picture in a tunnel called a 'shadow box.' This last-named monstrosity has almost disappeared; to come forth only now and then when paintings are brought out of old houses to be put up at auction sales. But the ornate and vulgar frame is with us still, casting its blight on whatever painting it can find to obscure and rob of its true effectiveness."

The situation has not changed much since Boswell's agonized outcry in the early twenties. While the public displays a greater and greater interest in paintings of all kinds—along with the same traditional neglect of good framing—examples of poor taste in framing continue to plague us.

What can be done about it?

A great deal!

The frame and its

relationship to the picture

There are four aesthetic reasons for framing a picture: to focus and limit the eye on the composition of the picture itself; to reinforce significant, but sometimes elusive, elements and color tones in the picture; to increase the size of the picture; and to serve as a transition between the picture and the wall behind it.

The most important consideration is the relationship of the frame to the picture.

It is an odd, but interesting, paradox that artists themselves have traditionally evidenced considerable frustration at selecting the proper frames for their works of art. One of the first in recent times to make a determined effort to overcome this helplessness was James Whistler, who was continually finding his delicately toned paintings hung in heavy, discordant frames. He was finally driven to making, designing and painting his own frames. To make sure that the owners of his paintings did not destroy the effect he wanted to achieve, by discarding the original frames and buying new ones, he started the practice of signing many of the frames with the familiar Whistler "butterfly." This added so much to the value of the entity, that few owners would even consider making a change of frame from that time on.

Another successful artist–frame-maker was the Boston landscapist Herman Dudley Murphy. "So successful was he in framing his own pictures," reported one critic, "that he was asked by brother artists to apply his ideas to other pictures."

Criticizing a tendency of the early twenties—and one that unfortunately still persists—Murphy, who was referred to as "the Dean of American Picture Framers," once said, "To frame pictures of different styles alike in one design of frame is to kill their individuality. They may look well in an aggregate, just as a regiment of soldiers looks well in uniform, but it should be remembered that the barber plays an important part in making the soldiers all look well in their uniforms. Imagine a person who has always worn his hair rather long, as Paderewski, for example, being put in the close-fitting uniform of our army. You would laugh at the incongruity, and feel the need of clothes of a different shape, or else the close cropping of his hair.... You may spoil absolutely the effect of a fine picture by an unsuitable frame, just as you may make an almost poor one look distinguished by a proper setting. Put a delicate, subtle Whistler nocturne in a glittering, heavily ornamented frame and hang it on a wall with a lot of other pictures and you will never see it. Put a simple flat frame of parallel lines upon a sumptuous Venetian subject of the style of Titian or Veronese and it would at once cheapen the picture and make it look almost tawdry."

It is easy to look at frames critically, or to quote established authorities (as above) on what *not* to do, but it is not so simple to discuss the subject constructively and suggest how to go about correct framing. Going back historically for a moment and approaching the subject from a "don't" point of view, one misconception about framing that has come down through the ages is that frames are *architectural* elements. While it is true, as will be discussed in the next chapter, that frames have to harmonize to some degree with the setting, they cannot primarily be considered from that viewpoint—that is, before the relationship of frame to picture has been carefully considered.

There was a time when a decorator, having once decided that the interior of a home should be "Tudor" or "Early American" or some other style, was then convinced that the furnishings and furniture—including all picture frames—should be in the same style. The effect can easily be realized if you will just picture a Louis XIV frame on a Grandma Moses primitive. Today, it is widely accepted that a tasteful interior can be a mixture of styles and periods, when there is a proper blending of elements and colors. Even so, many an owner of a fine painting, perhaps knowledgeable when it comes to the selection of art, will have such a vague concept of the art of framing that he will have only one criterion to guide him: the style of the furniture in the room. He therefore will let his judgment be guided far more by the traditional old architectural viewpoint than by the particular requirements of individual pictures.

Without knowing the first thing about the complexities of styles and periods in art history, you can come close to the selection of the proper frame just by studying the demands of the picture itself. Ask yourself whether or not there should be a marked transition between the picture and the molding. An oil that has great depth will often have that depth distorted if the molding is too close to the edges of the composition. The frame may tend to absorb the dimensionality of the painting. Therefore, by experimenting with different frames, you will begin to see that the ones with an insert or certain type of mat are more successful at retaining—and better yet, emphasizing—the depth of the painting.

For a picture that has this three-dimensional effect, it will usually prove most effective to have a molding that slants *inward* (toward the composition), regardless of the type of mat or insert, to enhance the dimension. Conversely, if the composition is flat, two-dimensional, as in the case of most paintings classified as "abstract art," moldings that are flat or slant outward (receding toward the wall) will be appropriate. They avoid the common mistake of using a frame to introduce depth to a picture that has little or no such dimension.

The matter of coloring is another point that can be of far greater importance than trying to match periods. Harsh coloring or shiny gilding on a frame, appropriate for some pictures, can easily drain much of the essence from a picture that otherwise would be lively and brilliant. A delicate overtone on the frame will serve to bring out subtle colorings within the composition. Here again, an insert or liner can help to separate related tones in picture and frame. Make a point sometime to study so-called "black-and-white" prints or antique engravings, or to examine closely paintings that are classed as "monochromatic." Instead of just one color, you will find the essence of several hues, all of which can be brought out and enhanced by the proper frame.

"Gold and black are always safe colors for pictures that have no real color," an artist said to me one day. Perhaps, but how much more effective to effect the skillful use of shades of brown or gray, or touches of metallic leaf that will strengthen the picture instead of merely border it!

Writing in *Plaisir de France* a few years ago, artist Jean-Pierre Guerin made the point that a good frame not only harmonizes with the picture but helps to develop and prolong the vision of the artist. Each element within the frame—size, design, color, makeup—should be thought of as something you can employ to "prolong the vision."

Take the matter of coloring. If a careful and considered study of a picture reveals delicate colors that might easily be overlooked by a more casual viewer, the frame-maker should consider what those colors, or their complements, could do for the picture when blended into the frame. On a bolder scale, think what a robust and "manly" frame can do to strengthen a picture like Modigliani's "Portrait of Cocteau."

Again, without getting into the concern over period and style, you can determine the proper size and weight for a frame by a simple, realistic consideration of the subject matter itself. Each picture, each composition has a definite "weight quality." Just as a matter of example, architectural subjects certainly tend to be far weightier than, say, even the boldest still life. Portraits of children are normally much more lightweight than portraits of their parents. A peasant scene is likely to be at home in a sturdy, substantial frame; whereas a composition showing ladies at a dance would be overpowered by this kind of a frame.

Another factor that may influence a decision about framing is the matter of *movement.* This is a difficult term to define, because there are so many different types of movement. The subject itself can be in motion, as in the case of John Steuart Curry's painting of three trapeze artists, "The Passing Leap." The colors can be lively, as in most of Gauguin's works. The lines can be in complex movement, as in Fernand Leger's painting, "The City."

At any rate, no matter what the type of movement, it is fairly safe to say that the more there is of it, the stronger the frame containing it will have to be. When you see a picture with a great many horizontal lines and conventional elements it is likely to require less strength in the frame than a picture that has diagonal lines, violent movement or other restless features.

The *mood* of the composition has to be considered as well. Romantic, gentle subjects call for more delicate frames than do those that are realistic and matter of fact. Surrealistic, fanciful subjects, such as those painted by Salvador Dali or Max Ernst, allow more inventiveness and daring than other types in the use of framing materials.

It has been mentioned that frames are useful in helping to increase the size of a picture. This is a feature, however, that has been rashly misused. You can find, without too much trouble, many pictures in homes, offices and even galleries that have been ridiculously overframed, simply because the wall space seemed to call for a larger artistic element than could be produced by the picture in a properly proportioned frame.

Another grievous practice is that of trimming down a picture to fit a frame already on hand or found in grandma's attic. Remember that a picture of any real value has a size, shape and proportion exactly determined by the artist himself. These qualities are as important to the picture, whether you like them or not, as the artist's choice of colors and the technique he has used in the rendering. To cut a picture to fit a frame is even more of an aesthetic crime than to select the colors for a matting strip because they happen to match the fabric of your new sofa!

Some of the "rights" and "wrongs" will be more easily understandable through a study of the visual examples in this book. The noted Degas once remarked to painter Moise Kisling, "The frame is the reward of the artist." To add a missing element to his statement, it should be pointed out that "a good frame is also the enduring reward of the owner of the picture."

Hans Memling's portrait of a Flemish man is at home in this simple wooden frame of a design used during the artist's lifetime. The texture enhances the painting.

This glaring, overdecorated frame, in brilliant gold and with a light insert,
attracts too much attention and drains the strength and color from the portrait.

Two approaches to framing a silk screen, Tugboat, *by George Picken.*
Frame, above, cramps the picture and has an overly plain, yellowish molding
that is unsympathetic to the subject.

Frame shows how a "minor" picture can be made into an important one by giving the subject "breathing space" and emphasizing the abstract pattern and depth of the work.

Two approaches to a still life by Jan Breughel. The hard, polished molding above is too thin and brittle for the subject. Its coloring clashes with that of the canvas.

Frame similar to ones used during artist's lifetime is ample and enhances the subject.

*The rustic feeling of Maine pines in this water color by William Zorach
is supported by the rough, straightforward frame. The linen mat and silver bevels
give fine accent to the blue of the sea.*

The hard Victorian frame is actually unrelated to the subject. The white mat is not only too harsh, but out of proportion.

TEN COMMANDMENTS FOR THE PROPER FRAMING OF PICTURES

1   The width and pattern of the molding must bear relationship to the design and "weight" of the picture. A painting with simple, uncomplicated design calls for a plain molding; a much-detailed composition is best balanced by a rich design in the frame, with ornamentation called for.

2   A receding molding (one slanting toward the wall) or a rather flat profile will suit two-dimensional paintings best.

3   A concave molding (one slanting toward the painting) will enhance the feeling of perspective suggested by a composition in depth.

4   Strong, bold patterns (such as in Roualt's paintings) demand powerful lines in the frame, to contain the composition.

5   A delicate, feathery, airy composition (such as a Vertes) calls for the same "frivolous" feeling in the frame.

6   A linear composition (such as a Feininger) calls for a repeat of this fine, lineal quality in the frame.

7   Inserts, or contrasting colors, will help to separate the ornamentation or pronounced color in a frame from those in the picture and will enhance the feeling of perspective.

8   Mats for watercolors and prints should be chosen to accentuate the significant colors. White is seldom ever right, because it tends to flatten the picture and darken it by contrast.

9   Only in the matter of glass protection do pastels and watercolors call for special treatment. A gouache can be as strong in color and pattern as any oil, and should be framed accordingly.

10   Key the colorings in frames to hues in the picture. A general guide is that warmly toned pictures (in which reds, browns and yellows predominate) are most appropriate in warm-toned frames; whereas cool colors (blues, greens, blue-blacks, whites) are likely to go best in frames that have silvery or similar cool tones.

The frame and its relationship to the background

There is an interesting and lively passage in Irving Stone's book, *Lust for Life,* that recreates a discussion between Georges Seurat and several other noted contemporary artists of his day. Seurat is speaking:

"….We get through with a canvas. Then what do we do? We turn it over to some fool who puts it into a hideous gold frame and kills our every last effect. No I propose that we should never let a picture out of our hands until we've put it into a frame and painted the frame so that it becomes an integral part of the picture."

"But, Seurat, you're stopping too soon. Every picture must be hung in a room. And if the room is the wrong colour, it will kill the picture and frame both."

"That's right. Why not paint the room to match the frame?"

"A good idea," said Seurat.

"What about the house the room is in?"

"And the city that the house is in?"

"Oh, Georges, Georges, you do get the damndest ideas."

"That's what comes from painting with your brain."

This little interplay of artistic exaggeration is quoted here as a way of pointing out that a picture frame has a responsibility far more complex than simply holding an object of art on the wall. In addition to serving its primary function of bringing out the best qualities in a picture, the frame has the secondary task of forming a graceful transition from surface to surface, regardless of what the situation, position or materials happen to be. Sometimes there must be a compromise, in order to achieve the best and most fitting overall presentation of the picture concerned. It would be unrealistic to assume that a picture can be wedded to the best possible frame in the frame-maker's studio and invariably be transported to its ultimate home with an absolute guarantee that it will be "right."

The question may, and frequently does, resolve itself into a debate as to which is more important, the painting or the decor of the room.

Looking at the relationships and values, we can find a number of instances in history, as well as in contemporary thinking, where pictures— even Old Masters—have been considered as a mere element of decor. For example, William Morris, the English writer, poet, artist, socialist, decorator and general critic of his day, was highly successful in pioneering a movement that looked upon painting as no more of an art than any other phase of architecture or interior decoration. It was perfectly valid, he contended, to design frames as part of the entire interior style, and then put paintings or other pictures in them, according to personal taste and desire.

Such thinking ignores the commonly accepted belief today that an appealing and tasteful interior decor does not necessarily have to fit a pattern, be determined by a formula or adhere strictly to one historical period throughout. "If a seventeenth-century frame turns out to be best for a picture, it should be framed that way, even in a modern room," says Bertha Shaeffer, owner of an art gallery and herself recognized as a leading decorator. As for groups of pictures, she adds that they can be hung together in *different* frames entirely, as long as there is some harmony of relationship.

People tend to become nervously confused when confronted with the problem of whether they should have frames that are "modern," "contemporary," "traditional" or "antique." To be clinical about it, contemporary frames certainly evidence as much relationship to good frames of other eras as the anatomy of man today does to his civilized forebears. A study of the makeup of a number of modern moldings will show that they are basically adaptations of conventional moldings of a past age. The quotation from *Ecclesiastes*, "there is no new thing under the sun," is as applicable to picture framing as it is to just about any other object on earth.

The appropriateness and modernity come, not through innovation, but through the fresh approach and natural application of elements and designs. That is one reason why it has been proven that furniture, furnishings and art of different periods can be mixed when properly integrated.

In the relationship of picture to surroundings, framing plays a decisive part in determining the *importance* of the picture. A heavy frame can make an oil painting more dominant than it otherwise would be. If it were appropriate to frame a print in a wood molding, and if that same molding were then used elsewhere in the room as an architectural feature, the picture would be less dominant than if its frame were unique to the surroundings.

The background helps to determine the strength and importance of the picture. A busy background, such as a flowery wallpaper, would not be appropriate for most pictures, with the possible exception of large, strongly colored oils. Even so, the hues in the background, unless carefully selected to complement the art, would prove distracting and create an undesirable restlessness. Surely here the frame should isolate and separate picture from background more noticeably and distinctly.

Texture makes a difference, too. Whereas a rough, burlap wall covering or Japanese grass cloth might be suitable behind large, strong-compositioned pictures, they might drain the beauty from more delicate pictures. The sheer starkness of smooth white plaster can help to add aesthetic impact to a dramatic scene; but it can also be overly dramatic if the subject of the picture happens to be fragile in nature.

A small frame can be made to look larger and a large frame smaller by the type and coloring of the wall. Contrasting colors will make the picture stand out; whereas harmonious colors will tend to absorb it, and reduce the apparent size of the frame.

With so many elements playing a part in determining the picture's importance, it is not hard to see that a collector has considerable flexibility in deciding what degree of strength the picture should have. It can be practically thrust out at the viewer, dramatized by the color and texture of the wall, and by the amount of space around it; or that same picture and frame can be absorbed, subdued—even destroyed—by the treatment of the surroundings.

An interesting and exemplary case history of picture vs. surroundings comes up in considering what to do about some of the current abstract paintings, which are two-dimensional and fairly simple and clean in composition. A few years ago, the problem of framing and hanging them was not so widespread because interiors tended also to be simple and uncluttered. Today, however, there is a definite trend toward the "rich" interior —rich in texture, in furnishings and in the number of objects scattered about.

I believe that these abstracts can often be appropriately framed in wide moldings of beautifully textured old chestnut, rather flat, with hand-carved designs inspired by archaic primitive, stylized patterns of African, Polynesian and Indonesian origin, combined with a definite, sharp outline around the canvas proper. These frames are entirely appropriate to the luxury of the surroundings, on the one hand setting off the art handsomely

How to frame a portrait in a setting whose very richness could detract from the painting.

Wall texture and coloring play an important part in determining the right frame.

and, on the other hand, isolating the paintings from the distracting features of other art in the room, large lamps or exotic plants.

Reproductions of art should be treated with as much respect as though they were originals when it comes to selecting frames. Naturally, most reproductions vary slightly from the originals in subtle toning, in "weight" and occasionally in size. The approach to framing, however, should be exactly the same—if the owner is really interested in the art to begin with.

Before leaving this discussion of the frame and its relationship to the picture and to the surroundings, mention should be made of one current school of thought, painful to many a frame-maker's ego. A few leading abstract expressionists, among them Mark Rothko, refuse to acknowledge that the frame has any place at all in their art. The Guggenheim Museum in New York is one of the chief exponents of framelessness; yet in a way the very architecture of the interior serves as a frame, enough so that it is hard to imagine the exhibits transported, frameless, to some residential interior without appearing a bit naked. Without some form of limitation, the paintings would undoubtedly clash with other objects in the room, or would at the very least have much of their strength sapped by conflicting patterns and colorations.

The argument has been set forth today that many abstract paintings are so huge that they are either, a) physically very difficult to frame, or, b) far too costly to frame. In either case, there is no sound artistic reason for omitting frames unless the surroundings can suitably serve the same purpose.

The rather widespread use of the "strip-frame" approach has a variety of reasons. But one of the most important stimuli for the frameless presentation of an exhibition was the example given by James Johnson Sweeney when he was director of the Guggenheim Museum in New York. As he made clear in the foreword of my book, *The Art and History of Frames*, his approach was misunderstood. The method of taping the edges of paintings, he wrote: "was never a flight from the frame, as it was too frequently misunderstood to be when it appeared as an innovation. Actually this apparently frameless essay at marrying the picture with wall was the outcome of a lengthy experimentation with frames of different widths, depths, colors and materials towards a means which best permits a white gallery wall to serve a double function, namely as a frame for each individual picture and at the same time as a frame for the total exhibition—unified background with the minimum of non-pictorial visual distractions."*

To quote him again, "And if the walls of our domestic interiors and art galleries are stark and austere and the furnishings sparse in comparison with those of a century ago, a frame to make the limits of a picture and to knit to its background is still essential."*

One other reason for the popularity of strip frames is certainly the economic advantage offered when framing a complete exhibition. But the uniformity can be deadly! It is so much more rewarding to give some individuality to the treatment of each painting, even if a certain basic similarity and relationship is generally effective in a gallery. However, in a home or

*Henry Heydenryk, *The Art and History of Frames* (James H. Heineman, Inc., New York, 1963).

office, these reasons cease to exist and only a stark, almost clinical or sterile interior would demand the limitations of the strip frame.

Truly modern moldings for the paintings of the sixties are available, making it easily possible to find a suitable frame to be the "fence against encroachment of its environment or a limit to its background and surroundings." We are not forced to limit our selections to strips of wood, metal or plastic, but can find modern forms that will function harmoniously and unobtrusively. Often a modest molding with an insert or liner will best fulfill the requirements of painting and surroundings—or a rather narrow band surrounded by flat, textured wood to provide the desired separation.

The frame that is right for a painting in isolation may not necessarily be the one that is right for the painting in any given setting. To demonstrate the principle of proper selection, Picasso's painting of the head of a woman was photographed in four different environments, in frames appropriate both to the subject and to the background.

On page 64, the painting receives unusual, but appropriate treatment, resting on an easel in a sharp, linear frame that is at home in a modern room overlooking the Pacific. In contrast, on page 65, the Picasso requires an antique eighteenth-century molding whose richness blends with the elegance of the room's eighteenth-century decor.

The clean, straightforward treatment shown on page 63 is also harmonious for the modern, uncluttered interior on page 66.
Placing a Picasso in an Early American setting is not easily accomplished.
Yet the treatment shown on page 67 is in good taste. The frame is American primitive, which suits both the subject and the surroundings.

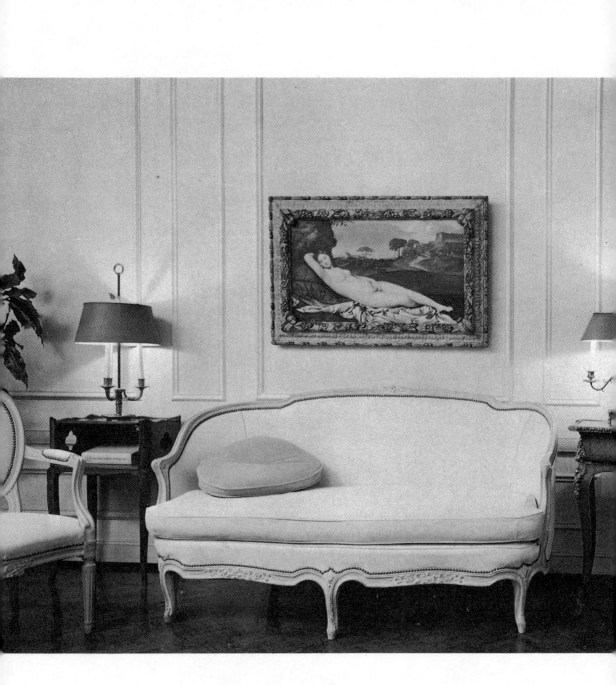

A reproduction of Giorgione's famous Reclining Nude *is shown in a distinctive French interior, framed handsomely in an original molding from the artist's period.*

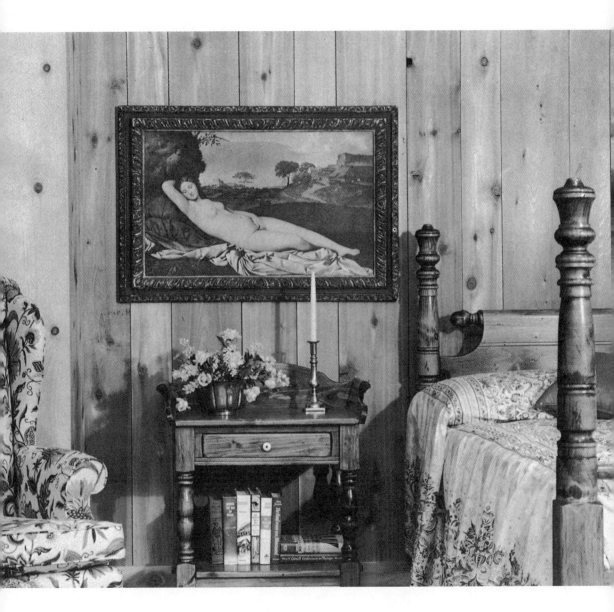

It is equally at home in an Early American bedroom, framed in a more severe Italian reproduction.

Proper lighting

In the Appendix to a scholarly work entitled *The Care of Pictures*, there is a section that reads as follows:

"Color Measurement. All measurement of visual tone in pictures is based on means to record the quality and quantity of light which can be reflected from a specific, uniform tonal area. The quantity is the total amount of light, regardless of color. Specific color is the quality of light reflected. A rough or approximate estimate of color measure for a given tone can be made by means of comparison with known samples...."*

The text refers basically to the use of color measurement in determining the condition of Old Masters, and is for the most part highly technical. The quotation is made here to lead into a discussion of the importance of proper lighting, not only so that viewers can better see framed pictures, but so that they can see the true colors, as applied by the artist, and with the values he intended.

*George L. Stout, *The Care of Pictures* (Columbia University Press, New York, 1959).

Picture frames bear a direct relationship to lighting.

For one thing, their shape, depth, coloring and reflective qualities can attract light to, or deflect it from, the surface of the picture. For another, their physical makeup determines how far out the subject hangs from the wall, and whether it is precisely perpendicular or slightly inclined. An important factor in the relationship is the nature and amount of color in the molding. This can effect subtle (and sometimes unwanted) changes in the tones of the picture.

Have you ever noticed how a soft, white sweater can take on a visible glow of color when the wearer has a brightly colored purse, or other reflective object in hand? Paintings can be equally critical, and with good or bad effect, depending upon the skill (or lack of it) that has gone into the selection of the frame.

It is universally, and traditionally, considered that the best light for paintings is *natural light,* or at least some form of illumination that closely approximates that of nature. The reasoning stems from the assumption that most good artists paint under a skylight, during the daytime, and preferably with the glass facing north. Hence, the colors and tones and shadings which they create under these conditions can be considerably distorted by artificial light, almost as much as though you were to view the work through a pair of tinted glasses.

It is therefore somewhat ironic that art in the home is hung in rooms that are occupied probably three-quarters of the time in the evening and where artificial light must be the prime consideration in the placement and treatment of the subjects. It is, in fact, rather astonishing that art can be properly appreciated at all in the home when you consider the multiple factors involved, such as differences in lighting fixtures, wide variations in the size, shape and coloring of rooms, the hundreds of types and wattages of bulbs available and individual ideas as to just how an object on the wall should be illuminated to begin with.

The Old Masters had no such problem. Artists knew exactly where their works were to be hung. In many instances they painted them right on the scene, frequently on the wall itself. Consider this passage from Heinrich Wolfflin's authoritative work, *Principles of Art History:*

"Light and shade, which cling to every form, become a painterly element at the moment at which they seem to have an independent import apart from the form. In classic style, they are bound to the form; in the painterly style, they appear unbound and quicken to free life. It is no longer the shadows of the separate pilaster or window-pediment of which we become aware, or, at any rate, not of these only. The shadows link up among themselves, and the plastic form can at times be quite submerged in the total movement which plays over the surfaces. In interiors, this movement of light can be carried on in oppositions of dazzling light and pitch dark, or tremble in merely light tones—the principle remains unchanged. In the one case, we must think of the vigorous plastic movement of Italian church interiors; in the other, of the flickering lightness of a very softly modelled rococo room..."

The Old Master, working right in this environment of "plastic movement," with its "oppositions of dazzling light and pitch dark" created his art for the scene itself. Today's painters usually have little idea where their works may end up—in a well-skylighted gallery, a darkly paneled drawing room of an old brownstone house, the modern living room of a ranch house in the suburbs. Therefore, it is entirely up to the purchaser to interpret the artist's intent and to determine the lighting conditions under which the picture will be shown.

Fortunately, today's technology has created artificial lighting whose values are close to those of daylight. Many galleries and exhibits successfully use forms of fluorescent lighting shielded by milky plastic to simulate the daylight which, architecturally, it may be impossible for the hall to have. While this effect is seldom achievable in the home, or in small, private collections, there are at least six methods of lighting that are practical for home use:

1   Overhead fluorescent, or other, lighting fixtures set into the ceiling to simulate a skylight.

2   Ceiling spotlights, with pinhole openings, that are unobtrusive, yet focus regulated light on the picture.

3   Wall spotlights, which are more noticeable, but that achieve the same effect as ceiling spots.

4   Long "pencil" or "finger" lights set in brackets *over* the picture, and usually attached to the frame.

5   Lights similar to No. 4, above, but with the brackets attached to the *bottom* of the frame.

6   "Heyden-Ray" frames that contain a series of thin incandescent bulbs concealed behind the molding itself, so that the surface of the picture is illuminated evenly and with no glare.

There has long been controversial discussion in the professional world of art about the best type of artificial lighting for home use. "*Over* the picture is generally better," says one school. "*Under* the picture is less obtrusive and gives the same effect," says another. "Lights never should be *on* the picture, but at a distance from it," insists a third group.

The only realistic approach is to experiment with a given picture, in its frame, until the right lighting effect is achieved. Some compositions are strengthened by a spot; other compositions require an absolutely even diffusion of light throughout.

Although the "Heyden-Ray" is my own invention, I do not recommend this kind of built-in lighting for general use. It is a kind of device that must be resorted to in, say, the case of an unusually dark painting hung in a dark location, or to give special emphasis to a painting—to underline its strength. There is no doubt that it—like a shadow box—produces an effect, but the danger is that the effect may be too artificial and detract from the refinement of subject and composition and color.

A minor point, but one that can often cause great detraction is the subject of wiring, when the light is attached directly to the picture. Nothing looks more incongruous than an object of fine art on a wall, trailing a drooping, sloppy light cord. At the very least, the cord should run straight down from the center of the picture, and be painted to blend as much as possible with the wall.

In the case of valuable paintings, proper lighting is not only important for the sake of illumination, but for the *protection* of the picture. As Stout says in his work on *The Care of Pictures*:

"....Excess light, especially direct sunlight or prolonged daylight, will fade certain colors and will hasten the darkening and weakening of the cellulose fiber in paper and fabric. Unbroken darkness causes discoloration of oils and augments the development of mold and fungi...."

Painting is housed in a frame without lighting.

Frame is a "Heyden-Ray," with built-in illumination.

The frame and its relationship

to various

media and materials

Thus far, the text has discussed framing broadly in relation to the "picture," with occasional reference to more specific media, or what Webster defines as "a representation, as of a person, group of objects, landscape, building, or the like, on canvas, paper, or other surface, produced by painting, drawing, engraving, photography, etc...."

Naturally, the medium used by the artist is one of the factors in determining the nature of the frame. This chapter is a cataloging of the most important and familiar media, with brief notes on guidelines for framing each kind. Comparisons are helpful in judging rights and wrongs. However, "The Ten Commandments for the Proper Framing of Pictures" listed in Chapter IV should always be taken into account. The following paragraphs are merely general comments.

OIL PAINTINGS: Commonly call for more substantial frames than other media. Moldings must have positive character, but should be simple in profile, with decorative motifs according to good taste. A major requirement is that the frame be strong mechanically, and rigid enough to hold the canvas securely on its stretcher, to prevent warping or movement of the canvas that would eventually crack the paint.

WATERCOLORS: Usually frames can be shallower, thinner and more delicate than with oils. Wider mats are the rule. An important current change over past concepts is that many watercolors are strong enough to take heavy, well-textured frames instead of just solid bands. Watercolors invariably require glass facing. French mats can occasionally be tastefully employed—mats that have decorative lines drawn around the "window." To prevent buckling, and consequent distortion of the image, most watercolors should be backed by rag board, plus a heavy cardboard.

PASTELS: Require frames similar to those for watercolors. The major exception is that some require little or no matting. Glass is required, but because of the smudging qualities of pastels, the glass should be separated from the picture by a thin, usually concealed, insert. Pastel is the most delicate of all media and will continue to shed tiny powder grains, even after coated with a fixative. Both pastels and watercolors require a strong sheet at the back of the frame to seal out dirt.

GOUACHE: Because of its physical kinship to watercolor, gouache requires much the same type of framing. However, since the colors are opaque rather than transparent, most gouaches will require heavier, stronger looking frames than watercolors. Some techniques for painting with gouache produce an effect so similar to that of some oil paintings that frame treatment should be more like that of an oil than a watercolor. Glass is normally required.

PRINTS: Lithographs, etchings, and woodcuts are commonly framed with narrow moldings of natural wood or black or dark gray. Stark white matting should be avoided; a soft or off-white is better. Matting can be quite wide and deep, sometimes with a pertinent inscription related to the print. Glass is necessary for protection. Some prints, such as etchings and lithographs, have what is known as "plate mark." This is a rectangular depression, running around the print, caused by the pressure of the printing plate at the time of publication. It should not be hidden by the mat. When prints are signed, the signature should also be given plenty of space. Prints that have marking on the reverse side can have clear acetate or glass on the back to show the marking whenever desired. Many contemporary prints are being created in such strong patterns and colors that they demand important frames, such as might be used on oil paintings.

ORIGINAL DRAWINGS: Their variety in style, size and medium (pencil, silver point, pen, quill, brush) as well as the color of the drawing and paper, make generalization extremely difficult. Fortunately much greater attention is now given to the framing of drawings than in the past. This increased interest by museums and collectors has brought about a more serious and careful approach to the choice of the color, texture and size of the matting, as well as the width, style and tonality of the frame.

PHOTOGRAPHIC PRINTS: Matting is all-important with photographs, which can be treated effectively in several ways. Often, prints are mounted directly on the mounting or backing, with no molding or glass. Others are best set off with some kind of molding—usually stained or natural wood, gold, silver or other metal.

Photographic portraits in color are becoming increasingly popular. They often hang in the living areas of a home, and they should, therefore, be framed with greater consideration.

MIRRORS: There are two types of mirrors—those with clear glass that are actually functional; and those which are antique (or purposely antiqued) and whose glass is in such condition that the overall purpose can only be decorative. In either case, mirrors structurally and aesthetically lend themselves to heavy frames. A mirror is one art form in which the frame itself can be dominant. It is also far more dependent than any kind of picture on the surroundings for its particular style. It becomes in effect, more a piece of furniture than an object of art; and since its surface reflects part of its surroundings, there must be a closer tie between its frame and the architecture than in the case of a painting. Highly carved and ornate frames that are too overpowering for pictures often make excellent frames for mirrors. The key to good taste here would be the relationship of the frame to the surroundings.

REPRODUCTIONS: The first rule for reproductions—whether of oil paintings, watercolors, pastels or prints is that they should be treated as originals when selecting the right frames. There are two slight differences. The first is an aesthetic one, that color values may not have the strength or dimension of the original, and hence would be appropriate in a frame that is not too heavy. The second is a mechanical consideration, that most reproductions have to be mounted (no matter what medium they represent) to prevent warping. In this case, they can be protected with varnish or sprayed lacquer so that no glass protection would be needed. The selection of frame is highly important here (especially when the subject matter is such that the viewer knows it could not be an original), to avoid any impression of cheapness.

There are two schools of thought regarding the framing of reproductions: the one expressed above, that they should be treated as originals and another viewpoint that, since reproductions represent a brand new craft, they should be framed only in the modern manner.

Artist and critic Frederic Taubes takes a practical, in-between outlook, particularly in the matter of oils: "In contrast to frames for most oil paintings—which frames in general retain a rather conservative character—frames for color reproductions are most effective when they are somewhat novel in design. Just how far to go in the direction of originality is a question of individual taste, and the decorator may always be at variance with the artist on this score.... The decorator will have in mind the total effect of the framed picture in relation to the decoration of the room, whereas a painter will look at it from the point of view of the painting alone, and will tend to be more conservative in his taste."

THREE-DIMENSIONAL OBJECTS: When it comes to other forms of art, such as sculpturing, frames are generally considered either completely unnecessary or else actual drawbacks. However, there are many instances in which framing can be employed effectively and tastefully. Several years ago, Salvador Dali's surrealist creations of precious stones were dramatically framed in moldings with built-in lighting. Jewels, coins, medallions, flat sculptures, valuable trophies—these are all examples of art and artistry that may be enhanced by the effective use of proper frames.

Whatever consideration one may give to the beauty, art and aesthetics of frame-making, much of any decision concerning the "right" frame must be based on purely *material* conclusions. Such practical elements as moldings and mats and inserts are as vital to the end result as are surface decorations and colors and other artistic embellishments. In this respect, a frame is like a piece of good furniture, which must have character and refinement, but which also must be physically suitable to its task without paying too much homage to the ravages of age, usage and hard times.

The selection of the molding by the frame-maker plays an important part in the finish and decoration applied. There are, for instance, certain types of ornaments that traditionally go with certain types of moldings—though there is no hard and fast rule. The diagram below shows the *profile* of a molding, to indicate more clearly the technical terminology, always useful in any discussion of framing with a frame-maker:

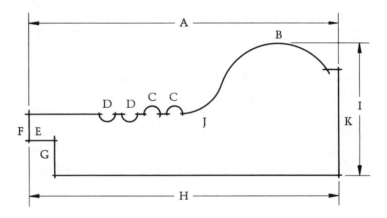

A Top or face of the molding
B Ridge or top
C Reeding (or beading)
D Fluting
E Lip of the rabbet
F Inside edge of the molding (next to the picture)
G The rabbet (where the painting or insert fits)
H Overall width of the molding
I Overall depth of the molding
J The profile (which may be of one molding or a combination)
K Outside edge of the molding (away from the picture)

Discussing moldings and materials brings us appropriately to the subject of *cost*. What is the right amount to pay for the proper frame?

There is an old story about the fourteenth-century painter, Giotto. He was commissioned by the Doge of Venice to do a painting, and a price was agreed upon. After the Doge received the painting, he sent it back to the artist to have him design and make a suitable frame. Giotto complied, with no objections, but when he rendered his bill for both works of art, the price had more than doubled!

Marie Antoinette is said to have once paid $3,000 for a frame—a sum that would equal about five times that today.

The costliest frame, however, is not necessarily the best. Frames for watercolors and prints are usually less, area for area, than those for oils. The average really good frame for a semivaluable oil painting today might realistically cost you about $85. It would be selected with care to fit (aesthetically and physically) an oil that you brought into the frame-maker's studio; it would use standard moldings, but hand-carved and finished on order for that painting alone. If you have a painting worth $800 to $1,000, it is not at all out of line to add 10 per cent to that value for a good frame.

The problem arises mainly with pictures of lesser value. If your painting is worth only $150 or $250 (or if perhaps its real value is speculative), do you still want to put $85—or anywhere from 35 per cent to 65 per cent of the cost—into the frame?

Moreover, the tremendous fluctuations in the value of paintings in the last twenty years make us realize that an inexpensive painting can well become very valuable. A well-chosen, well-made frame is, therefore, most important.

Good, ready-made frames are available at far less cost: from as low as $5.00 up to about $50.00. These are appropriate for some paintings, mainly those that fit some traditional school, or for established reproductions. However, buying frames, unseen, from a catalog can be highly unsatisfactory, unless the buyer knows exactly what he wants and what he will be getting. There is nothing like trying on a suit of clothes before you buy— and the same applies to a good frame!

Frames for mirrors can be larger and heavier and call more attention to themselves than can frames for pictures. This one reflects in the glass the images of a collection of picture frames which have been hung purely to display their own artistic qualities— without pictures. The frame on the mirror is an original, contemporary design.

*Left, color photograph, whose frame is heavy enough to provide solidarity
for the portrait within, but not overpowering.
Above, antique map framed in a simple wood molding that gives strength and depth
to an otherwise two-dimensional subject.*

Three-dimensional art can be framed tastefully and appropriately.
Above is a jewel cluster by Salvador Dali formally displayed in a frame with
built-in lighting. At right is an informal arrangement of medals and ribbons
in a deep, glass-protected frame. Sketch next to it, by Hirschfeld, is given character
by a decorative, but not too heavy, molding.

Some psychological observations on framing

"Ludwig Richter relates in his reminiscences how once, when he was in Tivoli as a young man, he and three friends set out to paint part of the landscape, all four firmly resolved not to deviate from nature by a hair's-breadth; and although the subject was the same, and each quite creditably reproduced what his eyes had seen, the result was four totally different pictures, as different from each other as the personalities of the four painters. Whence the narrator drew the conclusion that there is no such thing as objective vision, and that form and color are always apprehended differently, according to temperament."

Thus does Heinrich Wolfflin in his *Principles of Art History* demonstrate briefly the differences in psychological outlook among artists. In art books, in histories and in other works down through the ages, writers and authorities have constantly and zealously explored the psychological implications in paintings individually, in painting as a broad art, in sculpture, in music and in just about every other field of artistic endeavor. But few, if any, seem to have so much as given a thought to such implications as they relate to framing and the picture frame.

Why is a picture incomplete without a frame?

Why does an unframed canvas on a wall disturb the viewer?

Why does a frame in itself, with no picture contained inside, make you want to place something behind it—anything—to see what it looks like?

This chapter does not intend to furnish all the answers, but merely to make some observations that may be of interest in studying the nature of the picture frame and in applying principles right and wrong.

The English author, Gilbert Keith Chesterton, approached one point of view when he wrote, "Art is limitation; the essence of every picture is the frame." It was like the cover and binding of a book. One said what one had to say, had the thoughts compressed within the limitations of leather or cloth for posterity to ponder, and then went on to some other work.

Gertrude Stein was not so sure about any philosophy of limitation. "I like a picture, that is an oil painting to do anything it likes to do," she once said. "The first thing that ever interested me in that way as the picture moving was the Leonardo in the Louvre, the Virgin, the Child and Saint Anne...in this picture there was an internal movement, not of the people or light or any of these things but inside in the oil painting. In other words, the picture did not live within the frame, in other words it did not belong within the frame. The Cézanne thing was different, it went further and further into the picture the life of the oil painting but it stayed put.

"I have thought a great deal about all this and I am still thinking about it. I have passionately hoped that some picture would remain out of its frame, I think it can even while it does not, even while it remains there. And this is the problem of all modern painting just as it has been the problem of all old painting. That is to say the first hope of a painter who really feels hopeful about painting is the hope that the painting will move, that it will live outside its frame."

In her own way, Miss Stein has reflected a certain deep-rooted disturbance in the minds of many lovers of art: that there is a sense of security and well-being in seeing a picture strongly encompassed within its frame, or limitation, but that many pictures—like a tiger in a flimsy bamboo cage—do not seem to want to live within their prescribed confines.

One answer, though admittedly oversimplified, is that the *right* frame helps to make the viewer secure in his enjoyment of a picture, whereas the wrong frame can unsettle him by giving the impression that the picture is either, a) being throttled and overpowered, or, b) trying to bulge its way out of its surroundings.

Although the failure is not always easy to analyze, poor frames often arouse psychological misgivings when they are not in balance. Some painters are so concerned about this problem that they almost have an obsession about the relationship of the frame to one of their works. A number of years ago, the French painter Braitou-sala remarked about the frame, "The choice of its form, of its color and its material never leaves my thought while I am painting because it should be the prolongation of the work which is being born. One should construct the frame and the painting simultaneously so that they fuse so well in equilibrium that no one would think of separating them."

Portrait artist Albert Murray feels a great involvement with the frame, thinking of it as an extension of the painting. Often he will come into the frame-making shop to select a frame and then spend a great deal of time lovingly rubbing the molding with his hands until it has exactly the patina he desires—something that cannot be described or specified in technical or trade terminology.

Moise Kisling regarded frames as a kind of challenge. He liked nothing better than to select a superbly carved frame, set it up on his easel with a bare canvas inside and then reverse the accepted procedure by letting the frame dictate the composition and coloring of the painting he would execute.

One prominent art collector, Henry Pearlman, has been known to hang large expansas of wall with nothing but empty frames. When asked why he does this, he replies, "I think they're beautiful. They were done by hand, by real artisans who had *time*—not rushed like you and me." Pearlman's approach is both imaginative and inventive—he has one large frame that contains not one, but seven Cézanne drawings—but it evidences the appeal that frames hold for many people.

There is definitely an emotional quality about frames that give them personality and help to attract or repel the viewer. As an associate once put it in a light moment, "Frames can be sad or funny; voluptuous like a woman or severe like a Puritan preacher; warm and flexible as fine cloth, or cold and brittle as an icicle."

In studying frames, you can often feel some of the emotion coming through, thus adding to, or detracting from, the emotion of the picture within. A frame that is light, buoyant and lively quite naturally would fit a picture that has the same qualities, but would clash harshly with a picture that happened to be serious, somber, intellectual. Frequently a frame that is highly appropriate for a picture will have absolutely no appeal for a viewer, not because the frame is wrong, but because the viewer is not sympathetic with the mood and feeling expressed. The chances are, in a case like this, that he will not be greatly taken by the picture either.

There is one further function of the frame that might be referred to loosely as being "psychological" as well as practical, and that is its employment for protective purposes. Normally, glass is not used on a frame for an oil painting. However, in the case of an antique oil or one that, for any reason, has started to deteriorate, a special frame is required that does have glass on the front and a sealer on the back. "A great deal can be done to protect a picture by housing it in a suitable frame," explains Stout. "Observations over a period of about thirty years have given good reason to believe that paintings set into a frame which is, in effect, an airtight box have held their condition far better than similar works exposed to the air. Such a frame need not be heavy or cumbersome. It needs to have the glass sealed, to have the face of the picture some distance behind that, and to have an airtight backing. This framing keeps out dirt, it protects the picture from minor accidents, it keeps out water, and it reduces extreme and rapid changes of temperature and relative humidity."

This represents the ultimate in protection for a picture. Beyond that, it also furnishes a certain subtle and not easily defined sense of security that is appreciated by viewers as well as by the picture's owner.

Again, we see this symbolic representation of the frame as an element that protects fine art, because it is elusive, not easily defined and usually related to the emotions, flourishes best when it is securely confined, protected and psychologically satisfying.

Chronology

in its

proper perspective

"We are going to take a Velázquez and frame it in an adaptation of a Régence molding."

"I want you to see that drawing by Matisse, done in the 1920's. It is hung in a wide, simple nineteenth-century American frame."

Two decades or so ago, both of these remarks would have brought gasps of dismay from a large coterie of experienced art critics. You just did not consider anything but a Spanish Renaissance frame for a Velázquez! And whoever heard of putting a twentieth-century French work in an *American* frame designed for the preceding century?

Yet both of the works mentioned were at home in frames from different periods and different countries.

History runs in cycles, and every so often the so-called "purists" are in the vanguard, selling the notion that any kind of a mixture is bastardization or mongrelization and not suitable for the world of art. Fortunately, today, the trend is toward considering each situation individually, although many museums and collectors still do strive for strict historical accuracy when exhibiting paintings or any other art form.

Much worse than this striving for purism is the practice that has come into vogue again and again in the history of painting: discarding all of the old frames in a collection of Old Masters and replacing them with whatever happened to be currently in style. We have seen what resulted when Napoleon went overboard for Empire gold, and this unhappy act has many parallels in history—both before and after the Emperor's time.

Quite a few instances can be pointed out when good taste dictates that you almost *never* frame a good painting in a frame from its own particular period. One of the best examples would be the case of a masterful painting from the mid-Victorian period. It would be all but ruined today, as it probably was when it was painted, by being smothered in one of the plush, sentimental and multimoldinged monstrosities of the period.

Between the extremes of historical fussery and brash regimentation there lies a zone of reason that should guide any owner of fine pictures in the selection of framing: Frames for old pictures should be selected with a thoughtful respect for the period in which they were painted, with a consequent adherence to the spirit of good framing as practiced during that period. But allowances should also be made for current tastes, and to a certain degree technologies. If a certain motif popular in one era has since that time come to have a distorted, even objectionable, meaning, it obviously should not be used in a current design. The swastika is perhaps the most dramatic example—a perfectly honest, popularized design in ancient Greece, Persia and even back to the Bronze Age—that was turned into such a symbol of hate by the Nazis that its use in a frame molding would undoubtedly give the picture a meaning never intended.

Technology influences taste to the degree that an antique frame designed for use in a candlelit hall of 150 years ago would produce a somewhat different effect when hung in a modern salon. Does that old frame do the same thing for an antique painting as it once did? Or is it perhaps better to effect a modification, retaining the spirit and feeling, but possibly enfolding the composition more protectively and shielding it from some of the harshness that has crept into our modern decor?

In the matter of chronology, too little attention has been given to related factors: *geography* and *climate.* When you walk into a room, you enter from an outside environment. You may not think about it, but that environment definitely influences your interest in, and affinity for, various items, furnishings, furniture, art and other elements within an interior. Let us say that you have entered a living room after several hours spent outside, in desert country, in 100-degree heat. Your eye, your body, your thoughts will be attracted more by an airy, lightweight chair textured in cool green than in a dark, heavy, poreless armchair that looks as though it might stifle you in its grasp.

Conversely, if you walk into an inn after a cold drive through heavy snow, you are more likely to make your way to a dark, weighty table that is candlelit and has substantial chairs than to a wrought-iron ensemble near the sun porch that is surrounded by cool green plants.

Pictures and frames should be selected with at least some reflection on geographical and climatic environment. Subject matter, composition, style and other factors will be strengthened to a certain degree by the manner in which they are complemented by the surroundings—even the surroundings beyond the confines of the room in which they hang.

The fine art of hanging pictures

Not long ago, a man and his wife visited a prominent frame-maker to select exactly the right frames for five oil paintings and two watercolors. It took them something like two weeks and a dozen visits to the studio, before they were convinced that they had selected the proper frames.

The happy ending to this little story should have been that the couple proudly hung them in their duplex apartment where they were right at home and admired by one and all.

Not so.

As it turned out, the pictures had been purchased as part of a decorating project: to fill a large expanse of white wall in the living room, an area that had proven to be quite an artistic challenge. The wife had decided that "six or seven pictures" would do the trick, and the husband had further opined that the pictures would have to be genuinely fine art, expensive and superbly framed in the best of taste.

By the time the pictures had been duly arranged and hung they formed such a conglomeration of art that, instead of attracting admiring attention, they simply served as a kind of pleasant and colorful pattern, to which few guests ever paid any attention. Furthermore, two of the pictures were so high on the wall that they were properly viewable only when standing on a chair; one required a weed-picker's stoop to look at from a feasible angle; and none had proper lighting.

The moral of this little tale is that you can have the finest pictures and the most tasteful frames, but then throttle the effectiveness of works of art by hanging them, or grouping them, in a ridiculous manner.

There are two reasons for hanging pictures: The first, is to exhibit fine art properly, under circumstances where it can be studied and admired to the fullest extent; the second (and perfectly valid) reason is simply to provide a form of decoration. In the latter case, however, it is wasteful—indeed, an example of very poor taste—to sacrifice *valuable* works of art and carefully designed frames just to achieve a decorative effect that ranks no higher than that of the wallpaper or the pattern on the draperies.

As artist Van Day Truex once wrote, "Comparatively unimportant paintings and drawings can achieve gaiety and freshness when framed effectively with large mats, imaginatively colored and textured, or with cheerful moldings upholstered in anything from felt to chintz. But don't get your serious pictures mixed up with this philosophy...."

So group, group to your heart's content when you are hanging mere illustrations, but be careful when it comes to real art!

One basic dictate for hanging paintings precludes the possibility that you can group them properly, except in the most unusual circumstances: A good picture should be hung low. If you do not believe this, take a little time to observe where many people hang a picture—over the mantel. If the picture is a landscape, you will probably find that you cannot even look at it at all well without being clear across the room. Or, if you want to examine detail, you have to get up close and crane your neck.

Small pictures should be hung approximately at eye level, rather than lower, because their detail can be clearly seen without physical strain. No picture should be hung in a position where close inspection is impossible, which means that, whereas you might hang a large picture with large detail over a couch, this position would not be wise for a picture with minute detail, where the viewer would have to bend over awkwardly to try to inspect it at close range.

Remember, too, that pictures hung in a hall, where people are normally *standing*, require different positioning from those hung in a dining or living room where people spend most of the time *seated*.

Not many years ago, it was considered acceptable to hang pictures, particularly large, heavy paintings, from wire or cord that extended upward to the "picture molding" at the ceiling. In fact, just about every house built before World War II traditionally had picture moldings in the main rooms —and a good many still do. This method, while perhaps easier on the wall, distracts from the picture. In the case of large paintings, it emphasizes the physical weight of the whole, and often kills the effect of a composition that is light and airy. In the case of small paintings, such support looks incongruous.

The only way to affix a painting to the wall is in the most unobtrusive manner possible, by using picture nails and hooks—preferably two for each picture, spaced about three-fourths of the width of the entire frame apart, to prevent slipping into a crooked position. The wire and hooks should never be visible from any position a viewer might take.

When selecting the positions that various pictures will have on various walls, there are two other important considerations to bear in mind:

1   Have you allowed a realistic viewing vista? That is, can people see the picture at the proper distance, and with enough leeway so that someone really interested can look at the picture from both the right and the left, as well as in the middle? A good picture will bear observation from a dozen different positions, and some will reward the viewer by providing a slightly different effect from each viewpoint.

2   Have you taken the composition into consideration when selecting the location? Some compositions are more at home at the right end of a wall; some at the left; some in the middle. Probably the simplest example to demonstrate this principle is that of a portrait that is in profile. If the head is pointing toward the *left,* the frame should be hung somewhere to the *right* of the center of the wall, since the composition tends to give movement in the direction that the subject's eyes are looking. Such a picture might effectively be hung far toward the right end of the wall; but it would be disturbing at the left end, where it would seemingly be staring into the corner.

The final element for consideration is *space.*

A picture has to form a focal point, without distracting objects or decorations above, below, on either side or in front of it. Some paintings require more space than others, and the amount is by no means determined by the size of the frame. A quiet still life can happily occupy a smaller space than a colorful, lively carnival scene or an angry seascape. Subdued colors do not absorb as much of the surrounding wall as do bright and vibrant ones, as in the case of a brilliant abstract.

Whatever this book says, or fails to say, it is intended only as a guide, in a field that has been too little studied by the art world, and in which there are astonishingly few reference works of any length or in any language. When it comes right down to analyzing the art of framing, and to distinguishing the rights from the wrongs, the best general advice that can be given is absurdly simple in essence:

Try it out and see.

Check out one frame against another; style against style; period against period. Have the patience to live with a painting or other picture for awhile before taking what is really an important step with any real work of art—selecting the proper frame that will bring out its best qualities. And when it comes to selecting the frame, choose it with all the care and consideration that you used when selecting the picture in the first place.

WRIGHT   RONG..

Bibliography

Ayrshire, Williams, "The Philosophy of the Picture Frame," *International Studio*, New York, June, 1926, pp. 54-62.

Boswell, Peyton, "When the Frame Fits the Picture," *House and Garden*, February, 1921, p. 38.

Brooks, John, "Profiles: An Enhancing Adjunct," *The New Yorker*, April 27, 1963, pp. 49-81.

"Framing a Kuniyoshi," *Art in America*, No. 3, 1961, p. 51.

Goldstein, Harriet, and others, *Art in Everyday Life*, New York, Macmillan, 1954, pp. 442-444.

Guérin, Jean-Pierre, "A Chaque Tableau Son Cadre," *Plaisir de France*, January, 1958, pp. 42-45.

Heydenryk, Henry, *The Art and History of Frames*, New York, James H. Heineman, Inc., 1963.

Heydenryk, Henry, "The Art of Framing," *American Artist*, January, 1961, pp. 54-62.

Heydenryk, Henry, "Framing Right and Wrong," *Famous Artists Magazine*, Summer, 1955.

Hoffman, Raye, "How an Academic Approach Helps in Picture Framing," *Picture and Gift Journal*, October, 1956, pp. 12-26.

Keck, Caroline, *How to Take Care of your Pictures*, New York, Doubleday, 1958.

Landon, Edward, *Picture Framing*, New York, Tudor Publishing Company, 1962.

"Market Spotlight," *Interior Design*, February, 1958.

Reinhardt, Ed, and Rogers, Hal, *How to Make Your Own Picture Frames*, New York, Watson-Guptill Publications, 1958.

Roche, Serge, *Mirrors*, London, Gerald Duckworth & Co., Ltd., 1957.

Seckler, Dorothy Gees, "The Art of Framing," *Art in America*, Spring, 1958, pp. 67-70 and 81-84.

Stone, Irving, *Lust for Life*, New York, Doubleday, 1954.

Stout, George L., *The Care of Pictures*, New York, Columbia University Press, 1959.

Taubes, Frederic, *Better Frames for Your Pictures*, New York, The Viking Press, 1961.

Truex, Van Day, "How to Frame and Hang Your Pictures," *House and Garden*, December, 1946, pp. 127-133.

Wolfflin, Heinrich, *Principles of Art History*, Translated by M. D. Hottinger, New York, Dover Publications (paperbound, no date).

PHOTOGRAPHERS' CREDITS

Thomas Feist: Frontispiece, pp. 30, 72, 73
Unusual Films: p. 14
Charles Uht: pp. 26, 40, 41, 53, 61, 63, 64, 65, 83, 87
Stone and Steccati: pp. 55, 60, 62
Alfredo Valente: pp. 54, 86
Roy Stevens: pp. 28, 42, 43, 46, 47
Brenwasser: pp. 44, 45, 85
Rijksmuseum: pp. 15, 16
Boston Museum of Fine Arts: p. 17